W9-AAE-340

Savvy

Custom Confections

SWEET TOOTH!

NO-BAKE DESSERTS TO MAKE AND DEVOUR

by Jen Besel

CAPSTONE PRESS
a capstone imprint

Savvy Books are published by Capstone Press,
1710 Roe Crest Drive, North Mankato, Minnesota 56003
www.capstonepub.com

Library of Congress Cataloging-in-Publication Data
Besel, Jennifer M., author.
Sweet tooth!: no-bake desserts to make and devour / by Jen Besel.
pages cm. – (Savvy. Custom confections.)
Summary: "Step-by-step instructions teach readers how to make no-bake desserts, including parfaits, frozen treats, and more"– Provided by publisher.
Audience: Age 9-13. Audience: Grade 4 to 6.
Includes bibliographical references and index.
ISBN 978-1-4914-0860-5 (library binding)
1. Desserts—Juvenile literature. I. Title.
TX773.B48658 2015
641.86–dc23   2014001837

Editorial Credits
Ashlee Suker, designer; Sarah Schuette, photo stylist;
Marcy Morin, scheduler; Danielle Ceminsky, production specialist

Photo Credits
All images by Capstone Studio: Karon Dubke, except Shutterstock: Jaimie
Duplass, 37 (bottom), MaraZe, 47, margouillat photo, 31

Printed in the United States of America in North Mankato, Minnesota.
032014   008087CGF14

TABLE OF CONTENTS

MOUTHWATERING DESSERTS

...Whipped up by You!

Clear off the counter. Grab your tools. And get ready! You're about to whip up some spectacular treats—no oven required. Wishing for a cool treat for a hot day? Need an elegant dessert for that special event? Or do you just want to serve something unexpected? You've come to the right place.

You don't need to be a professional cook to make custom desserts. With a few ingredients and some simple steps, you can create your own beautiful masterpieces. And you won't even have to turn on the oven to do it.

So jump right in. What custom confection will you whip up today?

Convert It

The recipes in this book use U. S. measurements. If you need metric measurements, here's a handy conversion guide.

United States	Metric
¼ teaspoon	1.2 mL
½ teaspoon	2.5 mL
1 teaspoon	5 mL
1 tablespoon	15 mL
¼ cup	60 mL
⅓ cup	80 mL
½ cup	120 mL
⅔ cup	160 mL
¾ cup	175 mL
1 cup	240 mL
1 quart	1 liter
1 ounce	30 grams
2 ounces	55 grams
4 ounces	110 grams
½ pound	225 grams
1 pound	455 grams

Fahrenheit	Celsius
200°	90°
300°	140°
325°	160°
350°	180°
375°	190°
400°	200°
425°	220°
450°	230°

TOOLS

You'll need some kitchen tools to create mouthwatering treats. But don't worry. You probably have most of these in your kitchen already.

serving plates {1}

fine sieve {2}

cutting board {3}

muffin tins {4}

cupcake liners {5}

springform pan {6}

small melon baller {7}

lollipop sticks {8}

measuring spoons {9}

loaf pans {10}

spatula {11}

small paintbrushes {12}

candy thermometer {13}

bowls {14}

spoons {15}

cooling rack {16}

piping bags and tips {17}

electric mixer {18}

wax paper {19}

baking sheet {20}

serrated knife {21}

A TRIO OF Truffles

With three varieties of these tasty truffles, there's sure to be something for everyone.

Cake Batter Truffles

1 Beat the butter and sugar together. Blend in the vanilla. Add the cake mix and flour, and mix completely.

2 Beat in milk, 1 tablespoon at a time, until you have a dough consistency.

3 If desired, mix sprinkles into the dough.

4 Roll the dough into one-inch balls. Place the balls on a parchment-lined baking sheet. Refrigerate for 15 minutes.

¼ cup unsalted butter, softened

¼ cup granulated sugar

½ teaspoon vanilla extract

½ cup yellow cake mix

¾ cup ffour

3-4 tablespoons milk

2 tablespoons sprinkles, if desired

Cookie Dough Truffles

1 Beat the butter and sugars together. Add the flour and vanilla, and mix completely.

2 Beat in milk, 1 tablespoon at a time, until you have a dough consistency.

3 Pour in the mini chocolate chips. Mix the chips into the dough.

4 Roll the dough into 1-inch balls. Place the balls on a parchment-lined baking sheet. Refrigerate for 15 minutes.

¼ cup unsalted butter, softened

¼ cup granulated sugar

½ cup brown sugar

¾ cup ffour

½ teaspoon vanilla extract

3-4 tablespoons milk

½ cup mini chocolate chips

continued on next page

Dark Chocolate Truffles

1 Melt the dark chocolate according to package directions. Let cool.

2 Beat the cream cheese and sugar in a large bowl until smooth. Then stir in the melted chocolate and the vanilla.

3 Put the mixture into the refrigerator for at least one hour.

4 Roll the dough into 1-inch balls. Place the balls on a parchment-lined baking sheet. Refrigerate for 15 minutes.

6 ounces dark baking chocolate

4 ounces cream cheese, softened

1½ cups powdered sugar

¾ teaspoon vanilla extract

Decorating Truffles

1 Take the truffles out of the refrigerator and allow them to come to room temperature.

2 Melt the candy wafers according to package directions.

3 Gently drop one truffle into the candy melt. Carefully press the truffle into the candy with a fork to cover the top. Slide the fork under the truffle and slowly lift it out of the candy. Slide the fork over the lip of the bowl to scrape off any excess candy. Then gently place the covered truffle back on the baking sheet.

4 If desired, cover the truffle with nuts or sprinkles while the candy is still wet. Repeat the process with the other truffles.

5 Let the truffles set for at least 30 minutes.

6 If you wish, melt a second color of candy wafers. Drizzle the candy over the truffles. Let set for another 30 minutes.

candy melting wafers

chopped almonds or walnuts

sprinkles

STUFFED
Strawberries

Take strawberries from sweet to spectacular with this recipe. Pipe in a tangy cheesecake filling for an easy but elegant treat to eat.

12

fresh strawberries, washed and
patted dry

1 8-ounce package of cream
cheese, softened

½ cup powdered sugar

1 teaspoon vanilla extract

2 ounces dark chocolate,
chopped into small pieces,
if desired

1 Cut the stems off all the strawberries.

2 Cut the tips off the strawberries so they can stand upright. Place the strawberries on a baking sheet.

3 Scoop out the center of each strawberry, leaving a hole for filling. }

4 Beat the cream cheese, sugar, and vanilla until fluffy.

5 Put the cream cheese mixture into a piping bag.

6 Fill each strawberry with cream cheese mixture. }

7 If you want a chocolate drizzle, put the chocolate in a microwave-safe bowl. Melt the chocolate in the microwave, stopping every 15 seconds to stir.

8 Once the chocolate is melted, drizzle it over the strawberries. }

FROSTY FROZEN
Cakesicles

These frozen cheesecake treats will be a hit with kids of all ages.

Mint Chocolate Cakesicles

1 Crush the sandwich cookies. Put ½ cup of the crumbs into a large bowl. Pour the remaining crumbs into another bowl and set aside.

2 Combine the cream cheese, yogurt, sugar, milk, peppermint extract, and a few drops of green food coloring in the bowl with the ½ cup of crumbs. Mix until well combined.

3 Pour the cream cheese mixture into ice pop molds, leaving 1 inch at the top.

4 Mix the reserved cookie crumbs and butter together. Press 1 tablespoon of the cookie mixture into each mold.

5 Press a craft stick into the center of each mold. Put the molds in the freezer for at least six hours.

36 chocolate sandwich cookies, divided

1 8-ounce package cream cheese, softened

¼ cup plain Greek yogurt

¾ cup powdered sugar

⅓ cup milk

¼ teaspoon peppermint extract

green food coloring

2 tablespoons melted butter

continued on next page

Strawberry Cakesicles

1 Blend the cream cheese, yogurt, sugar, milk, and strawberries until well combined.

2 Pour the cream cheese mixture into ice pop molds, leaving 1 inch at the top.

3 Mix the graham cracker crumbs and butter together in a small bowl. Press 1 tablespoon of graham cracker mixture into each mold.

4 Press a craft stick into the center of each mold. Then put the molds in the freezer for at least six hours.

1 8-ounce package cream cheese, softened

¼ cup plain Greek yogurt

¾ cup powdered sugar

⅓ cup milk

¾ cup frozen strawberries

½ cup graham cracker crumbs

2 tablespoons melted butter

Change It Up

You can make frozen cheesecake pops in all kinds of flavors. Try these other variations.

Switch the frozen strawberries for another kind of frozen fruit. Blackberries, raspberries, or blueberries are great options.

Dip the frozen pops in melted chocolate to make a candy shell.

Follow the strawberry cakesicle recipe, but replace the plain yogurt with peach yogurt and add diced peaches.

Divide the cream cheese, yogurt, sugar, and milk into three bowls after mixing. Add a different frozen fruit to each bowl. Blend the contents of one bowl. Then fill each mold one-third full. Repeat with the other two bowls, layering the different fruit flavors in the molds, and then freeze. You'll end up with layered cakesicles with three fruit flavors.

4 cups water, divided

2 boxes blue gelatin

1 box yellow gelatin

1 cup sweetened condensed milk, divided

2 envelopes unflavored gelatin

8 gelatin snack cups, any flavors

GELATIN *Art*

Turn gelatin into a work of art. The layering takes a little time, but the results will be well worth the wait.

1 Spray an 8-inch square baking pan with nonstick spray. Bring 3½ cups of water to a boil in a saucepan.

2 Empty one package of blue gelatin into a bowl. Pour in 1 cup of boiling water. Stir until the gelatin is dissolved. Pour the hot liquid gelatin into the baking pan. Put the pan in the refrigerator for 20 minutes.

3 While the blue gelatin is cooling, pour ¼ cup of the yellow gelatin into a bowl. Add ¼ cup of boiling water to the bowl, and stir until the gelatin is dissolved. Then add ¼ cup of condensed milk and mix to combine. Pour this mixture into the pan over the blue layer. Refrigerate for another 20 minutes.

4 Pour ½ cup cold water into a bowl and sprinkle the unflavored gelatin on top. Let it sit for two minutes.

5 Pour 1 cup of boiling water into the unflavored gelatin. Stir until the gelatin is dissolved. Add ½ cup of condensed milk and stir. Let this mixture sit until it reaches room temperature.

6 Run a knife around the edges of the premade gelatin cups to pop the gelatin out. Cut the gelatin into cubes. Then sprinkle the cubes on top of the yellow layer in the pan.

7 Pour the white gelatin you made in step 5 over the cubes in the pan. Refrigerate for another 30 minutes.

8 Repeat step 3 to create a yellow layer on top of the cubes. Then repeat step 2 to create a blue layer on top. Once it's done, cut the gelatin art into squares or other shapes before serving.

Edible Cups of *Mousse*

White chocolate mousse is delicious on its own. But put the mousse in candy cups, and you have a dessert that's hard to beat.

1 bag candy melting wafers, any color

2 4-ounce packages white chocolate instant pudding mix

2½ cups milk

1 16-ounce tub whipped topping, thawed

toasted hazelnut pieces *(See page 44 for recipe.)*

1 Place the melting wafers in a small zip-top bag. Leave the bag open and microwave on the defrost setting for 30 seconds. Squeeze the melted candy to one corner. If the wafers are not soft yet, microwave on defrost for 30 seconds more. Snip off the corner of the bag.

2 Place a mini muffin liner in each cup of a muffin tin.

3 Pipe about 2 teaspoons of melted candy into the bottom of one liner. Use a small paintbrush to coat the sides of the liner with melted candy. Make sure all parts of the liner are coated.

4 Repeat step 3 until you've done all the liners in the pan. Then put the pan with candy-coated liners in the freezer for at least one hour.

continued on next page

5 Pour the pudding mixes into a large bowl. Add the milk. Stir until the ingredients are well mixed.

6 Gently fold the whipped topping into the pudding. Chill this mousse mixture in the refrigerator for at least 1 hour.

7 Take the cups out of the freezer. Gently peel away the paper liners.

8 Fill a piping bag with the mousse mixture. Pipe mousse into each candy cup.

9 If you wish, top each cup with toasted hazelnut pieces.

Custom Tip

You could also use white, milk, or dark chocolate for the candy cups. Just melt the chocolate according to package directions. Then paint the cups as you did in steps 3-4.

Edible Flowers

Don't use flowers from your backyard for any desserts. They could have poisonous pesticides on them. Go to a flower shop, and ask the florist for pesticide-free edible flowers.

1 cup granulated sugar

½ cup corn syrup

½ cup water

food coloring

candy flavoring oil, any flavor

small edible flowers, such as violets, lavender, violas, or marigolds

EDIBLE FLOWER Lollipops

These treats are both gorgeous and tasty. They make great gifts too. Simply wrap them in colorful cellophane and tie with a ribbon. Give someone's day a "pop" of sweetness.

1 Spray a lollipop mold with nonstick cooking spray.

2 Mix the sugar, corn syrup, and water in a saucepan. Clip a candy thermometer to the side of the pan. Bring the mixture to a boil without stirring.

3 When the mixture reaches 250°, add food coloring until you get the desired color.

4 Continue to cook the mixture, without stirring, until it reaches 300°. Then take the pan off the stove.

5 Stir in two or three drops of flavoring oil.

6 Quickly pour the mixture into the shapes of the mold. Place a flower or two on each shape. Use lollipop sticks to gently press the flowers down into the hot candy. Then press the sticks into the candy, using the stick holes in the mold. You'll need to work fast because the mixture will harden quickly.

7 Let the lollipops sit for about 15 minutes.

8 Pop the lollipops out of the mold.

LOVELY LAYERED Parfaits

Whether you're craving chocolate or need a fruity treat, these cups of layered goodness will be just what you're looking for.

Chocolate Parfaits

1 Turn a glass or small jar upside down. Press the glass into the chocolate cake to cut out circles.

2 Make the pudding according to package directions.

3 Drop two large spoonfuls of whipped cream into each glass. Then press a cake circle into each glass on top of the cream.

4 Sprinkle in some toffee pieces. Pour chocolate syrup on top. Then drop two more large spoonfuls of pudding into each glass.

5 Repeat steps 3 and 4 until you've filled the glasses.

1 8-inch square chocolate cake

butterscotch instant pudding mix

whipped cream *(See page 45 for recipe.)*

toffee pieces

chocolate syrup

Raspberry Parfaits

1 Cut the pound cake in half horizontally so you have two thin cakes. Turn one parfait glass or small jar upside down. Press the glass into the pound cake to cut out circles.

2 Whisk the jam and water together in a small bowl.

3 Drop two large spoonfuls of whipped cream into each glass. Then press a cake circle into each glass.

4 Drop two large spoonfuls of jam on top of the cake pieces. Add three or four raspberries on top of the jam.

5 Repeat steps 3 and 4 until you've filled the glasses.

1 10-ounce frozen pound cake, thawed

8 tablespoons raspberry jam

2½ tablespoons water

whipped cream *(See page 45 for recipe.)*

fresh raspberries

TASTEFUL *Tiramisu*

Tiramisu is an elegant, delicious dessert. Its creamy layers are a beautiful way to end a meal.

¾ cup whipped cream *(See page 45 for recipe)*

8 ounces mascarpone cheese, softened

3 cups brewed coffee, cooled

about 30 ladyfingers

cocoa powder

1 Line a loaf pan with plastic wrap, letting the plastic hang over on all sides.

2 Gently mix the whipped cream and mascarpone cheese together.

3 Pour the coffee into a bowl.

4 Dip an entire ladyfinger into the coffee. Then lay it in the loaf pan. Repeat with six more ladyfingers, arranging them on the bottom of the pan.

⌒continued on next page⌒

5 Spread one-third of the whipped cream mixture over the cookies.

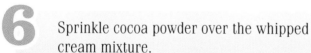

6 Sprinkle cocoa powder over the whipped cream mixture.

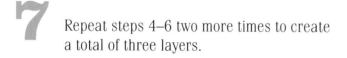

7 Repeat steps 4–6 two more times to create a total of three layers.

8 Cover the pan with plastic wrap and refrigerate overnight. When you're ready to serve, lift the tiramisu out of the pan using the plastic wrap. Remove all the plastic wrap before slicing.

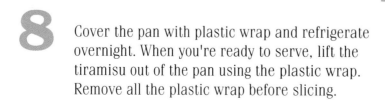

Change It Up

You can do all kinds of things with tiramisu.
Try these variations.

Use pound cake instead of ladyfingers.

Make mini tiramisu in small glasses. Cut the ladyfingers or pound cake to fit inside the glasses. Then layer the cake and filling until the cups are full.

After putting the coffee-dipped ladyfingers in the pan, spread a light layer of raspberry jam over them. Then spread the whipped cream mixture over the jam.

Instead of dusting the dessert with cocoa powder, drizzle chocolate syrup over the whipped cream.

Just before serving, top the tiramisu with chopped candy bars or fresh berries.

STRIPED ICE CREAM Cake

With ice cream, pound cake, and jam, this dessert is layered with tasty flavors. Even better, you won't have to heat up the kitchen making it.

1 loaf frozen yellow
pound cake,
slightly thawed

1 loaf frozen chocolate
pound cake,
slightly thawed

½ cup strawberry jam,
divided

2 pints vanilla ice cream,
divided

1 pint raspberry sorbet

1 Line a 9x13-inch baking pan with plastic wrap.

2 Cut both loaves of pound cake into 1-inch slices. Arrange the yellow slices in the pan so they cover the bottom. Set the chocolate slices aside.

3 Spread ¼ cup of jam on the pound cake layer. Then spread one pint of vanilla ice cream over the jam. Put the pan in the freezer for 30 minutes.

4 Spread a pint of sorbet over the ice cream layer. Freeze for another 30 minutes.

5 Spread the last pint of ice cream over the sorbet layer.

6 Spread the remaining jam on the chocolate pound cake slices. Put the cake slices on the ice cream layer, jam side down.

7 Cover the pan with plastic wrap. Then place the pan back in the freezer for at least eight hours.

8 Once the cake is frozen, turn the pan over on top of a cutting board, and let the cake slide out. Remove the plastic wrap. Cut off the edges to make them neat. Then cut the cake into slices.

Custom Tip

Beat the sorbet and ice cream
with an electric mixer to make
them easier to spread.

FROZEN LEMONADE
Poppers

You won't be able to eat just one of these tangy frozen treats—and neither will your guests!

1. Crush the graham crackers into fine crumbs.

4 sheets graham crackers

2 tablespoons melted butter

1 tablespoon granulated sugar

8 ounces whipped topping, thawed

1½ cups sweetened condensed milk

¾ cup frozen lemonade concentrate, thawed

fresh blackberries, washed and patted dry

2. Stir the cracker crumbs, butter, and sugar together in a small bowl.

3. Spray a mini muffin tin with nonstick cooking spray.

4. Spoon 1 heaping teaspoon of the cracker mixture into each muffin cup.

5. Press the cracker crumbs down firmly to cover the bottom of each cup. A small glass can help with this part. Then put the muffin tin in the refrigerator while you work on the filling.

6. In a large bowl, fold together the whipped topping and condensed milk. Gently stir in the lemonade concentrate.

7. Spoon 1 tablespoon of the whipped topping mixture into each muffin cup. Then cover the tin with plastic wrap, and put it in the freezer for at least eight hours.

8. When you're ready to eat, run a knife around the edge of each treat to pop it out.

9. Top each bite with a blackberry.

CHOCOLATE ALMOND Dessert Bars

Combine almond flavor and chocolate for a treat that's perfect for a picnic or a party. Put it all on a pretzel crust, and you have a dessert that won't last long.

2½ cups crushed pretzels

½ cup granulated sugar

1½ cups melted butter, divided

½ teaspoon almond extract

3 cups powdered sugar

3 tablespoons milk

½ cup butter

2 cups milk chocolate chips

candy melting wafers

whole almonds without shells

1 Mix the crushed pretzels, sugar, and 1 cup melted butter together in medium bowl.

2 Spray a 9x13-inch baking pan with nonstick cooking spray. Then firmly press the pretzel mixture onto the pan bottom.

3 Beat ½ cup melted butter, almond extract, powdered sugar, and milk together.

4 Pour the powdered sugar mixture over the pretzel crust. Place in the refrigerator for at least one hour.

Custom Tip

If you're out of pretzels, use graham cracker crumbs instead.

continued on next page

5 Heat ½ cup butter and chocolate chips together in the microwave, stirring every 20 seconds until melted.

6 Melt ½ cup candy wafers according to package directions.

7 Spread the chocolate over the powdered sugar layer in the pan. Drop small spoonfuls of the melted candy on top of the chocolate. Pull a butter knife through the melted candy and chocolate to create swirls.

8 Before the topping sets, quickly press almonds into the bars. Space them evenly so you can cut the dessert into pieces later. If you wish, melt a few more candy wafers, and drizzle the candy over the almonds.

9 Refrigerate the bars for at least 30 minutes.

Change It Up

You can change up the flavor of these bars in a snap. Try these variations.

Replace the almond extract with orange extract.

Sprinkle chopped walnuts or pecans on top instead of almonds.

Use mint chips instead of chocolate chips, and replace the almond extract with vanilla extract.

Chop your favorite candy bar into small pieces. Instead of nuts, sprinkle the candy pieces on top.

ROLLED WAFER COOKIE *Cake*

Turn a simple cream cheese and pudding dessert into an edible masterpiece. Lovely and tasty, rolled wafer cookies add a special touch and a delicious crunch.

1. Cut the cookies into 2½-inch pieces and set aside. Put the leftover 1-inch pieces in a zip-top bag and crush them.

2. Spray a springform pan with nonstick cooking spray. In a small bowl, combine the cookie crumbs, graham cracker crumbs, and butter. Then press the mixture onto the bottom of the pan.

3. In a large bowl, beat the cream cheese and sugar until smooth.

4. Add the pudding mixes and milk to the cream cheese mixture. Beat until mixed.

5. Fold the whipped cream into the pudding mixture.

6. Spoon the cream cheese mixture over the crust. Cover the pan with plastic wrap and refrigerate for at least six hours.

7. Just before serving, remove the sides of the pan. Arrange the 2½-inch cookie pieces around the dessert and press gently into the sides.

8. Garnish the cake with chocolate curls.

1 can rolled wafer cookies

½ cup graham cracker crumbs

¼ cup melted butter

1 8-ounce package cream cheese, softened

1 cup granulated sugar

2 3-ounce packages instant pudding mix, any flavor

3 cups whole milk

1 cup whipped cream *(See page 45 for recipe.)*

chocolate curls *(See page 46 for recipe.)*

OOEY, GOOEY
Turtle Cake

Bring the magic of turtle candies to the table with this terrific spin on terrific flavors.

1. Pour 2 cups of chocolate chips into a large bowl.

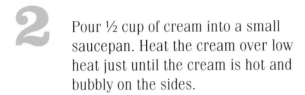

2½ cup semisweet chocolate chips, divided

1 cup heavy cream, divided

11 ounces melting caramels

2 teaspoons sea salt

2½ cups pecan halves

2. Pour ½ cup of cream into a small saucepan. Heat the cream over low heat just until the cream is hot and bubbly on the sides.

3. Pour the hot cream over the chocolate. Stir until the chocolate is melted and the mixture is smooth. Let the chocolate cool for two hours.

4. Spray a springform pan with nonstick cooking spray.

5. Whip the cooled chocolate mixture for about one minute. Then pour it into the pan.

6. Put the caramels, salt, and ½ cup heavy cream into a microwave-safe bowl.

7. Microwave the caramels until melted, stopping to stir every 30 seconds.

8. Pour the caramel mixture into the pan over the chocolate layer. Sprinkle the pecans and ½ cup chocolate chips on top of the caramel layer.

9. Let the cake rest at room temperature for at least four hours. Before serving, remove the pan's outside ring. Transfer the cake to a serving plate.

Toasting Hazelnuts

Toasted hazelnuts will make any treat extra special.
Making them does require a little baking. But the process
is so easy, and the result is so good.

3 cups water

4 tablespoons baking soda

1 cup hazelnuts

1. Bring 3 cups of water to a boil in a saucepan.
Then carefully add the baking soda and nuts.
The mixture may bubble, so be careful.

2. Let the nuts boil for three minutes. Then pour them
into a colander and rinse well with cold water. Use your
fingers to slip the skins off the nuts.

3. Lay the peeled nuts on paper towels and pat dry.

4. Preheat the oven to 350°. Spread the nuts evenly on a
baking sheet. Bake them for 15 minutes, stirring every
five minutes.

5. When they're done baking, pour the hot nuts into a
bowl and allow them to cool. Then chop the cool nuts.

Whipped Cream

1 cup cold heavy
whipping cream

$1/3$ cup powdered sugar

pinch of salt

1. Pour the cold cream into a large bowl.

2. Add the sugar and salt to the cream.

3. Use an electric mixer on low speed to whip the cream. Keep mixing until the cream forms stiff peaks. As soon as you see the stiff peaks, stop whipping.

Variations

You can flavor whipped cream for a fun twist. Add a tablespoon of cocoa powder for chocolate whipped cream. For a lemon treat, add a tablespoon of lemon juice. You could also use extracts such as peppermint or vanilla.

Chocolate Curls

3 ounces semisweet baking chocolate

1 tablespoon shortening

1. Put the chocolate and shortening in a small microwavable bowl. Heat it for 20 seconds on high heat. Stir the mixture with a fork. If the chocolate isn't melted yet, heat it for another 20 seconds.

2. Place a baking sheet upside down on your work surface.

3. Pour the chocolate onto the center of the baking sheet.

4. Spread the chocolate out on the baking sheet to make a thin layer.

5. Put the chocolate-covered baking sheet in the freezer for two minutes.

6. Take the sheet out of the freezer. Scrape a metal spatula along the baking sheet, pushing the chocolate into curls.

Chocolate Tips

Here are just a few more tips for making the best chocolate curls.

Make sure your bowl, baking sheet, and other tools are completely dry before you start. Even just a drop of water can make the chocolate seize, and it won't curl.

Melt the chocolate slowly for the best results.

Use toothpicks to lift the curls. The heat from your fingers can melt the chocolate and ruin your curls.

You can use white or dark baking chocolate too.

Glossary

DRIZZLE (DRIZ-uhl)—to let a substance fall in small drops

EDIBLE (ED-uh-buhl)—able to be eaten

GARNISH (GAR-nish)—something added to a dish for flavor or decoration

SEIZE (SEEZ)—when chocolate lumps up into a thick, dry paste

Read More

Besel, Jen. *Baking Bliss!: Baked Desserts to Make and Devour.* Custom Confections. North Mankato, Minn.: Capstone Press, 2015.

Krumsick, Cristina Suarez. *No Bake Makery: 80 Two-Bite Treats Made with Lovin', Not an Oven.* New York: Grand Central Life & Style, 2013.

Rau, Dana Meachen. *Eye Candy: Crafting Cool Candy Creations.* Dessert Designer. North Mankato, Minn.: Capstone Press, 2013.

Internet Sites

FactHound offers a safe, fun way to find Internet sites related to this book. All of the sites on FactHound have been researched by our staff.

Here's all you do:

Visit *www.facthound.com*

Type in this code: 9781491408605